30 Days in Genesis
Part Two

A Journey: from Patriarchs to Providence

By: Leah Lively

For
My Creator God

<u>Welcome</u>

Hello friend, I cannot believe you are holding my fourth study in your hands. I am truly honored. My first study on the book of John was released in 2019, and my second on the book of Acts was released in 2020. I have enjoyed the process of exploring books of the Bible and developing these studies to help you crave to study God's word without being intimidated or overwhelmed.

I decided to write my third study on the book of Genesis because we do not follow only a New Testament God. We follow the God of creation who created you to have a holy relationship with you. As followers of Christ, we cannot forget the purpose for which we were created.

My first two studies cover an entire book of the Bible within thirty days, breaking down each chapter into easy to read and process pieces. The book of Genesis is fifty chapters. To provide a thorough study of Genesis within a thirty-day time frame, I chose to write the Genesis study in two parts. Part one covers Creation to the departure of Jacob to Paddan-Aram. Part two begins with Jacob wrestling with God and ends with the Israelites residing in Egypt under Joseph's care.

I hope you are encouraged in your journey through Genesis. I pray as you learn more about God, you will see his might, power, and inconceivable love for you. Grab part one of the study when you are finished to read from creation and the beginning of the patriarchs.

I am praying for you.

Leah

<u>Completing this Study</u>

I have several goals for writing this study:

- To give an introduction to studying the Bible

- To show a less intimidating approach to studying the Bible

- To make the Bible accessible for busy parents and families

- To encourage you to discover what God wants to tell *you* through scripture

At the beginning of each day's study, I encourage you to pray, inviting the Holy Spirit to show you what you need to see. For example: "Dear God, reveal your truth to me. Help me to understand your words. Amen." The format is simple for one reason, while my words and interpretations can guide you, only God can say to you what He wants *you* to hear. Whatever God says will align with scripture. It will not be the opposite.

Next, read the entire scripture for that day (***written at the top of each page***). The Bible was written in large sections, not verse by verse. You can gain a better understanding when you read a full chapter. I recommend getting a hard copy of the Bible (see "Helpful Links and Resources"). You can also go to several sites for online Bibles. There are also a variety of free Bible apps.

Then, complete the day's study. You may need a notebook or place to write answers to the **Journal** sections. I used the English Standard Version Bible (ESV) in my study writing, but feel free to use your preferred version.

Finally, end in prayer, using the sample prayer at the end of each day or praying a prayer of thanks for God's truth.

What is Genesis?

The book of Genesis is the first book of the Old Testament of the Bible. Genesis means "beginning" as it gives an account of the origin of all things within a span of two thousand three hundred sixty-nine years. It is the first of five books written by Moses, the prophet who received the Ten Commandments from God on Mt. Sinai in the book of Exodus. A Hebrew raised in Pharaoh's palace, Moses wrote these books using God's guidance, along with trusted sources and documents. They are known as the Pentateuch (Greek), Torah (Hebrew), or the Law.

Besides the creation of the world, through Genesis, we are confronted with the entrance of sin into the world and man's constant battle with it. God refreshes the earth through a massive flood but provides a way for communion with him through obedience. Abraham and Sarah, an aging childless couple, are promised descendants who number the stars and who will eventually have land to call their own. They learn the meaning of obedience through a circumcised heart as God gives them a son to carry out the covenant. The promised son Isaac and his wife Rebekah birth twins, two nations who war in the womb and the battle for a birthright blessing. Jacob, the twin to receive God's covenant blessing, struggles with a deceitful father-in-law as he waits seven years to marry the woman who won his heart. Jacob becomes "Israel," the father of the twelve tribes of the Jewish nation. These twelve tribes are rescued by a brother who shows mercy when they deserve death. Joseph gives their families a home in a land of plenty for four hundred years.

The fulfillment of the Abrahamic covenant does not happen in Genesis, but we can watch the growing faith of the Patriarchs as they walk in obedience to a Holy God.

The Character of God

"In the beginning, God..." Genesis 1:1

As you walk through the book of Genesis, I pray that God reveals parts of himself to you. In the stories within these pages, God makes himself known individually and personally. Use this page to make notes as you discover the character of God.

<u>Day 1: Genesis 28:10-22</u>

✓ Pray ✓ Read ✓ Take Notes

Jacob, grandson of Abraham and son of Isaac was over forty years old when he left for Padaan-aram. Jacob's twin brother, Esau, threatened to kill him after Jacob deceived his father and received his brother's birthright and blessing. Their mother Rebekah urged their father Isaac to send Jacob to her family to find a wife, thus preserving his life. They did not want Jacob to marry the women in their region, as Esau had done. The women in their area belong to families who worshipped idols and not the God of their forefather Abraham.

28:10   Jacob left _______________ and went to _______________.

Read **Genesis 12:1-4**

Where did Abram (Jacob's grandfather) live?

What did God tell Abram when he was there?

Jacob is going to the place where his grandfather first received his calling from God. The place where God told him to **go**, become a **great nation**, receive a **blessing** and a **great name**.

It is the first time we find Jacob alone and away from family. The quiet darkness is the perfect opportunity for God to move and speak into Jacob's life.

28:11-13 Jacob laid down one night with his head on a stone. *What* did Jacob see? *Who* did Jacob see? *What* did Jacob hear?

In many Bible versions (i.c. English Standard Version), the same world is repeated three times: Behold

Behold means "pay attention" and it is said three times because God is trying to make a point.

28:12 and 13 – Behold, there were *angels*. Behold, there was a *ladder*. Behold, there was *God*.

What did God tell Jacob?

28:15 - *Behold*, I am with you and will keep you wherever you go, and will bring you back to this land. For I will not leave you until I have done what I have promised you.

28:16   "Surely the ___________ is in this place, and I _________ _________ _________ _____."

28:17   What emotion did Jacob feel?

This *fear* was reverence and awe. Jacob was in shock. His eyes were opened to the power and presence of God, for the first time in his life. The God of his grandparents and parents became *real* to him.

What do you think the *ladder* represented?

God does not want to remain at a distance in your life. He wants a relationship with you. The ladder creates a bridge from heaven to earth. Allowing all of us to be in relationship with God.

<u>Journal</u> – Have you had a dream or a moment where your eyes were opened to the majesty and awe of God? Where you saw evidence of his hand on your life and details of the situation? What feelings did it bring to you? What did you see and hear?

28:18 What did Jacob do with the stone?

The stone that held his head while he slept became an altar of worship, representing how Jacob would build his life from this point. The dream demonstrated God's *omnipresence*. God was with Jacob no matter where he traveled. Ancient peoples during that time believed their gods were regional and did not travel to other areas. Egypt gods only existed in Egypt. God's presence was with his people as he moved them from region to region.

28:19 He called the name of that place ___________________.

Bethel means *House of God*.

28:20-22 What vow did Jacob make to God?

     If...

     Then...

This dream and physical act of creating an altar would be a point in Jacob's life that he could remember where God made a covenant with him and Jacob made a vow in return. In the coming months and years, Jacob would look back on this night and draw strength and confirmation the Lord was with him.

God gives us moments like this; reminders that He is with us in the chaos of our lives. When God reveals himself to you, however he chooses (through a dream, scripture, song, prayer, etc.), write down every detail. There will be times in your life when the enemy wants you to forget and question, "Did God actually say…?" (Genesis 3:1)

Jacob is about to enter a period that will make him question everything in his life, but he can remember this dream, this covenant, and this altar where God became more real to him than he ever had been in his life.

PRAY: *"If God will be with me and will keep me in this way that I go…" Genesis 28:20 – God, open my eyes to see how you reveal yourself to me. Help me to remember those moments during my dark days, confirming you are with me every day. AMEN*

<u>Day 2: Genesis 29:1-30</u>

✓ Pray ✓ Read ✓ Take Notes

Jacob has arrived in the region of his mother Rebekah's family, Paddan-aram. He is in search for his uncle Laban's family.

Read **Genesis 25:27**.

>What did Jacob grow up doing?

Living in tents – means that he stayed around their home, tending to the flocks of sheep and cattle. His forty years of tending to his family's livestock will be a vital skill from this moment forward.

29:2-3 What did Jacob observe when he arrived?

Jacob was a shepherd, so he was accustomed to being watchful of flocks, water, and surroundings. His life's passion was with the tents and the livestock.

29:4-6 Immediately, who does Jacob encounter?

Jacob disagreed with the time they were coming to water their flock. He did not realize the shepherds were waiting for Rachel so the stone could be removed for sheep, then put back in place.

29:9-10 What did Jacob and Rachel have in common?

29:10-11 What was unusual about their meeting?

Before Jacob's eyes, God was fulfilling his covenant from Genesis 28:15. Quickly finding his uncle's family as well as his beautiful cousin, Jacob knew that God was "with him" in this place.

29:13-14 How did Rachel's father (Rebekah's brother) Laban react?

29:15   After one month, Laban asked Jacob what question?

29:16-17 Describe Laban's daughters:

Leah

Rachel

Other translations describe Leah as having soft, weak, or tender eyes. Some believer her eyes were blue as compared to the typical brown eyes of the people in that region. The Hebrew word is *rakkoth* which translates to "tenderhearted", describing her inward appearance. Rachel, on the other hand, was immediately described by her outward appearance "lovely in form".

29:18-20 What did Jacob want? What agreement did he make with Laban?

What does Laban gain in the agreement?

The seven years of labor was a bride price. A portion of what is paid in a bride price is kept as a nest egg for the daughter. In seven years of labor, Laban would have a heavy sum to set aside for Rachel. Laban gets to keep his shepherdess and gains an experienced shepherd which would benefit him monetarily. At the end of seven years, Jacob expects his demands to be met. Laban makes plans for the wedding, but his deception begins.

29:23-25 What happened on the wedding night? What was Jacob's reaction?

Brides are heavily veiled until the morning after the wedding night.

29:26 What excuse did Laban give?

29:27 What was the new agreement?

Jacob was now married to ________________ who was given her servant________________ and married to _____________ and given her servant _________________.

In **Genesis 27:1-13**, Jacob played a role in his own act of deception. What happened and who was involved?

While God promised to be with Jacob and bless him, God does not ignore the sin in Jacob's life.

<u>Journal</u> – Ask God to help you recognize unacknowledged sin in your life. What sin God has brought to your attention that was a roadblock to your journey of faith? What is something you must surrender to God regularly? Write a prayer giving that sin to God.

Sin must be reconciled before you can move toward holiness.

PRAY: *"Why then have you deceived me?" Genesis 29:25 – God, open my eyes to the sin in my life. Help me surrender my sins and temptations to you so they do not become a trap as I move toward the life you have called me to. AMEN*

Day 3: Genesis 29:31-30:24

✓ Pray   ✓ Read   ✓ Take Notes

Jacob got a taste of his own deception and was now married to two sisters, while preferring the younger over the older. Just as his mother preferred him over his older brother, he preferred the younger sister over the older.

Jacob's preference for Rachel was not mild.

29:31   How do you think Leah was treated? What did the Lord do for her?

Rachel was _____________________.

Read **Genesis 11:30** - Who was also barren?

Sarai became Sarah and was married to Abraham. God called Abraham to be the father of a nation with offspring numbering the stars. At the time, Sarah was barren with no possibility of offspring. God opened Sarah's womb and gave her a son named Isaac, Jacob's father. A barren woman birthed the child of promise.

29:32-35 Leah was the first to produce offspring for Jacob. Fill in the chart with details about each son:

	Name	Details
1st		Born of affliction; hoped Jacob would love her
2nd		
3rd		
4th		

29:35 Leah's response in the birth of Judah was different than the
       others. Write her response here:

Leah waited until the birth of her fourth son to "praise the Lord".
With each birth prior, she focused on her pain. This time she
focused on God. Winning Jacob's favor became an idol for Leah,
where she placed her complete focus. Finally, she placed her focus
on God.

<u>Journal</u> – What are you experiencing now that you can lay aside and
"praise the Lord"? In a time of great sorrow, praise may be the
furthest from your mind and your heart. *Lament* is another form of
praise. It praised God for his faithfulness and steadfast love even
though you may be grieving a loss. This is the best time to praise
God anyway. Write a prayer of praise, thanking Him for his
promises and steadfast love.

Leah ceased giving birth. Rachel's grief led her to a decision of
desperation. Producing offspring was the main role of a wife to
continue the family line. The inability to have children was a tragedy
for the family.

30:1   How did Rachel feel about her sister?

        Who did she blame?

30:2   How did Jacob respond?

Jacob knew he was not responsible for her inability to have children.
He remembers the story of his father Isaac and grandmother Sarah.
Jacob knew God's promise and accepted He was in control.

30:3-4 What did Rachel suggest?

Read **Genesis 16:2** - Who did Sarai (Jacob's grandmother) blame?
        What did she suggest to Abram?

Both Jacob and Abraham knew God's promise of a nation. They did
not know how that would happen. At this point, the descendants of
Jacob totaled four sons. This was hardly a nation that numbered the
stars or dust of the earth.

Rachel felt shame for being unable to give children to Jacob. She
was desperate to erase that shame any way she could. Her servant
would have to help her. Because Bilhah "belonged" to Rachel any
offspring she produced would also be considered Rachel's.

Make notes about Rachel and Jacobs's sons born to Bilhah (30:6-8):

	Name	Details
5th		God has judged me
6th		

<u>Journal</u> – Envy and shame are emotions no one wants to feel. Sarah and Rachel took control of their situations when they knew their future was in God's hands. People today cover up their negative emotions with drugs or alcohol, binge watching shows or overeating. Think about how you choose to cope with negative emotions. What would be a better alternative?

Jacob's attention turned away from Leah and their sons. Leah's focus on Jacob became an idol for her again.

30:9 What did Leah do to "win" her husband's attention?

Make notes about Leah and Jacob's sons born to Zilpah (30:11-13):

	Name	Details
7th		
8th		

Reread 30:2 – Who is responsible for Rachel's fertility?

The competition between Rachel and Leah continues in the next scene. Rachel attempts to manipulate God and both women continue to manipulate their husband.

30:14-15 What did Rachel request? What agreement was made?

The aroma of mandrakes was believed to induce feelings of love and encourage fertility.

How often do we do the same? "Maybe my circumstances will change if I do a. b. or c." Rachel has spent years trying to alter her situation. Accepting God's will is not always easy. Many women struggle to conceive, while others seem to have the exact number of children they desire. Some couples have beautiful marriages while others end in divorce.

The problem is where we place our *focus*. Do we focus on circumstances we cannot control or on God who knows the best for our lives?

Instead, Leah is the one to get pregnant from the agreement three more times. Put the details here (30:17-21):

	Name	Details
9th		
10th		
11th		

30:22 Write the verse here:

We do not know how much time has passed, but long enough for Rachel to watch the women in her family become pregnant ten times. More than ten years of swollen bellies surrounding you can make any barren woman bitter. Rachel is hurting, ashamed, angry, and envious. God hears and remembers her by opening her womb.

30:23-24 Write the details of Rachel's birth here:

	Name	Details
12th		

Each child was named specifically and describes what Rachel and Leah were experiencing at the time. Take time to look up the names in a Bible dictionary or biblehub.com. The names will be significant in later chapters as their characters develop.

Rachel yearned for more children. Her name for Joseph carried that desire, "he increases".

PRAY: *"Then God remembered Rachel and God listened to her..."* *Genesis 30:22* – *God, thank you for remembering my cries and listening to my prayers. Help me to focus on you and your will for my life instead of the circumstances I cannot change. AMEN*

Day 4: Genesis 30:25-43

✓ Pray   ✓ Read   ✓ Take Notes

By this point, Jacob had served his father-in-law/uncle for twenty years. God gave Jacob a family and offspring, but Jacob still worked *for* Laban. He did not have any possessions for his livelihood.

30:25-26   What did Jacob request of Laban?

30:27-28 Immediately, Laban seemed compliant. What did he acknowledge and what did tell Jacob to do?

In **Genesis 24:50-58** we get our first introduction to Laban as Rebekah's (Jacob's mother) brother. What agreement did he make then attempt to change?

Laban is not a man of integrity. He tries to keep his sister from leaving to marry Isaac, despite acknowledging that it is in God's plan. When Jacob requested Rachel's hand in marriage, Laban secretly gives him Leah. Jacob knows not to fully trust his father-in-law.

30:29-32 Jacob reminds Laban of what he had done for the family's prosperity since his arrival. What wages does Jacob ask for?

V33   Write this verse here and underline the word having to do with *integrity*.

30:35-36 Laban agrees with Jacob's wages but has his own plan.
        What does Laban do?

Laban steals from Jacob, then leaves so he will not be caught. Jacob is fully prepared for Laban's deception.

Jacob was a highly experienced shepherd. He knew how to create a stronger and weaker flock. Relying on an ancient method, Jacob was able to produce an abundance of strong spotted cattle, sheep, and goats, increasing his wealth exponentially in a short time.

In **Matthew 25:14-30**, Jesus tells the parable of the talents. Three servants are entrusted with some of their master's money as he goes away on a journey. When the master returns, two men had doubled the money. They are praised by the master, deemed good and faithful, and given more money to oversee. The third is afraid and hides the money. This is seen as wicked and lazy by the master, so the servant is sent away.

<u>Journal</u> – When God blesses you, it is your job to care for what God has given you. Think about how God has provided for you and blessed you. How have you cared for those blessings? How have you used your gifts to serve God?

PRAY: ***"So my honesty will answer for me later..."*** *Genesis 30:33 – God, help me serve you with honesty and integrity as I care for the blessings and gifts you have entrusted to me. AMEN*

<u>Day 5: Genesis 31</u>

✓ Pray ✓ Read ✓ Take Notes

Trouble is brewing as Jacob's brothers-in-law complain about Jacob's prosperity. Laban has treated Jacob poorly. It was time for Jacob to return home.

31:3   What did the Lord command Jacob to do?

And I _________ ______ ______ ______.

Jacob calls Rachel and Leah into the field to explain the situation to them.

31:5-9 What did Jacob tell them about their father?

What did Jacob tell Rachel and Leah about God?

The girls were used to their father's deception. This was nothing new. Now they would be witnesses to God's provision. This was completely new.

31:10   Describe the details of the vision God gave to Jacob.

31:12   ______ ______ _______ _______ all that Laban is doing to you.

Jacob is seen by an omnipresent God.

31:14-15 How did Rachel and Leah feel deceived by their father?
          What did they tell Jacob to do?

Their father spent their portion of the bride price that he should
have reserved for them.

For the first time, the quarreling sisters have united against their
father, placing their trust in their husband and God.

Without informing Laban, Jacob left with the livestock, his family,
and possessions to go to the land of Canaan.

31:19   What did Rachel take from her father?

Laban had given Rachel no possessions as well as taken her wedding
week from her. The little gods called "teraphim" were used in
household worship were linked to divination and prosperity.
Laban's father and Abraham (Jacob's grandfather) were brothers.
Interestingly, Laban acknowledged Jacob's God in several instances
yet continued to worship these statues.

Look up the following verses. How does Laban acknowledge the
God of Abraham, Isaac, and Jacob?

Genesis 24:31

Genesis 24:50-51

Genesis 30:27

Many people believe in God and speak of God, but do not have a
relationship with God. There is no fruit in their life that comes from
a knowing God and walking with him daily. Laban's character is
proof that he does not know God and does not allow God to guide
his life. Jacob, while not perfect in his youth, developed honesty
and integrity as his walk with God grew stronger.

Journal - In **Matthew 7:15-20**, Jesus talks about false prophets,
those who speak about God, but do not have the fruit or evidence
that they know God. Have you seen someone's character change
because of their relationship with God? Have you been able to
discern the strength of someone's character because of their lack of
spiritual fruit?

Laban discovered that Jacob left and pursued him for seven days.
Something pivotal happened in his relationship with God.

31:24 What happened when Laban was pursuing Jacob?

        God made himself known to Laban.

31:26-28 Laban caught up with Jacob. What did he claim Jacob did
        to him?

Laban informed Jacob that God told Laban not to *say* anything to
Jacob, good or bad. Laban did not obey God. Laban also blamed
Jacob for stealing the household gods.

31:31   What defense did Jacob give to Laban's claims?

Not knowing Rachel stole the gods, Jacob also reassured Laban that
the thief would be punished if they were found.

31:33-35 Laban searched the tent for his household gods. How did
        Rachel hide them?

It is possible that Rachel took the gods because she thought they
would help her family.

31:36-41 Now away from Laban's control, Jacob shares his
        frustrations. What claims did Jacob make about his father-
        in-law?

31:42   Jacob brought glory to the One who deserved it. Who
        protected Jacob and gave Him prosperity? Who was on
        Jacob's side?

________ saw my affliction and the labor of my hands and
________________ you last night.

31:43   While Jacob gave all glory to God for his success and
        prosperity, how did Laban respond?

Even a vision from God did not put Laban's focus on anyone except
himself.

31:44-50 Laban has not gotten his way, so he suggests a covenant
        with Jacob.

        What did they build?

        It was named "the heap of witness" or "watchtower".

        What did it represent?

        What did Laban require of Jacob?

Laban continued to talk, stressing that the pillar would be the
marker between the two of them. They would not cross the pillar to
the other side to do one another harm or God would judge them.
The God Laban talked about but did not know.

Jacob stayed quiet during the ceremony. Perhaps his actions spoke
louder than Laban's words.

31:53-54 What did Jacob *do*?

This was a sacrifice of peace, a meal between family.

Jacob had a relationship with the God of Abraham and his father Isaac. They instilled fear and reverence in him. He was confident in God because he had a relationship with him. Laban would not distract him from what God called him to do in verse 3: "Return to the land of your fathers and to your kindred, and I will be with you."

The next morning, after saying good-bye to his daughters and grandchildren, Laban returned home to Haran.

PRAY: *"But the God of my father has been with me" Genesis 31:5 –* *God, remind me that you have always been with me. During joy and sorrow, you are with me, guiding me. AMEN*

<u>Day 6: Genesis 32</u>

✓ Pray ✓ Read ✓ Take Notes

Jacob is on his way home. He is not anticipating a joyful reunion. When he left home twenty years ago, he went under the guise of going to find a wife. Jacob left to save his life.

*To understand the events and emotion of Genesis 32, you may need to review significant verses of Jacob's past.

In **Genesis 25:23**, Rebekah (Jacob's mother) is experiencing a difficult pregnancy. God reveals to her that two nations are in her womb. More significantly, "the older shall serve the younger." In their culture, the firstborn son is given the birthright and a blessing from the father. The birthright entitled the son to inherit the family business and fill the patriarchal role in the family. God's message to Rebekah was that the younger would gain the birthright of the Jewish nation.

Later in **Genesis 25**, Esau gives his birthright away to Jacob for a bowl of stew. Esau did not value his role in the family. Jacob felt entitled to it. As their father neared the end of his life, he called Esau (his favorite son) into his tent and asked for a special meal to give Esau his blessing. As Esau was hunting for and preparing the meal, Rebekah rapidly disguised Jacob (her favorite son) with Esau's clothing and smell to trick her blind husband into giving Jacob the firstborn blessing.

The plan is carried out. Jacob is given his father's blessing over Esau. In his anger, Esau threatens to kill Jacob. Isaac and Rebekah send Jacob to Haran to find a wife among Rebekah's family.

Now that Laban has returned home, Jacob can focus on the journey ahead of him.

32:1   Who appeared with Jacob on his journey?

What impact do you think this had on Jacob as he was preparing to meet his brother for the first time in twenty years?

32:3-5 Jacob sent messengers to his brother. What did he tell Esau?

Why do you think he shared details of his prosperity?

Jacob received his father's birthright and blessing, but God had confirmed to Jacob that it was God's blessing that was intended for him. Jacob had no intention of returning home to take anything from Esau.

His messengers told Jacob that Esau was coming to meet him with four hundred men.

32:7-8 Then Jacob was greatly ________________.

        How did Jacob respond at first?

32:9-12 Jacob then turned to God in prayer. From his prayer, how
        has Jacob changed from the arrogant deceiving brother
        twenty years prior to the man in this point of the story?

In Genesis 28:15 and 31:3, what does God promise Jacob?

What evidence throughout these chapters as proven God is with
Jacob?

Jacob had success and prosperity in Haran, despite Laban's
deception and Jacob's past sin. God has proven he is with Jacob.
God even sent angels to Jacob at this point, but Jacob remains
fearful of Esau and seeks God in prayer.

Journal – Fear is inevitable. Throughout the Bible, there are over
300 verses with the command "Do not fear" or "Have courage".
Many of those commands are followed with the reassurance of
God's presence. How has God proven his presence to you in your
past so that you can be reassured of his presence in your future?

32:13-20 What did Jacob send ahead as a peace offering to Esau?

32:24   And Jacob was ________________________________.

At the beginning of our first week of study, we met Jacob, alone in the wilderness at the beginning of his journey. In his solitude, God came to him in a vision, promising him a nation of people and land that belonged to them. At the end of our week (and twenty years later), Jacob is alone, and God finds him in the wilderness. Their first meeting was in a dream. This meeting is more physical in nature.

32:24-31 What happened to Jacob physically?

What happened to Jacob spiritually?

God also changed something about Jacob. What did he change? Why?

Abram became Abraham "the father of a nation."
Sarai became Sarah "the princess of a nation."
God told Abraham and Sarah to name their son Isaac, "laughter."

32:28   Jacob became Israel, which means:

Read **Genesis 25:26**
        What was Jacob doing when he came out of the womb?

Whether instigating, initiating, or immersed in the middle Jacob was surrounded by a struggle his entire life. His struggle was over. He saw God face to face. Relationship struggles, financial struggles, and spiritual struggles can take their toll.

Jacob not only fought, but prevailed. Jacob was an overcomer.

We do not overcome struggles without battle wounds.

PRAY: *"For I have seen God face to face, and yet my life has been delivered." Genesis 32:30 — God, thank you for reminding me that with you I do not need to struggle alone. You have my life in your hands. With you I will overcome. AMEN*

<u>Day 7: Rest/Catch-up</u>

Feel free to catch-up on lessons or review to prepare for the upcoming week. You can also take time to record character traits of God on page 6.

This past week showed us two men on two ends of the spiritual spectrum. They came from the same lineage, but one man focused on himself while the other focused on God. One man was loud and deceptive, while the other was reserved and discerning. One man cheated in his relationships while the other upheld his integrity with those around him.

Jacob was not always kind and righteous. This week we will see him have to face his past, but this time, he has God on his side.
The God who was made real to him in his dream at Bethel remained faithful to him in the twenty years he spent in Haran. God remains with him as he confronts his past deception.

You are never too far from God's reach. We may walk away from God, but when we quiet our lives, stepping into the wilderness, God will often find us there. He does not always speak in a dream or vision, but God will make his presence known when it is time.

Just as God transformed Jacob's life, he can do the same for each one of us. All that asked of you is to surrender and focus on God's will for your life. That is something Laban could not do. His narcissistic behavior cost him greatly. He may have been left with plenty of income because of Jacob, but he lost his daughters and grandchildren. Never owning up to his sin created a stone barrier between him and those he loved.

A surrendered life is not easy. You will not have all the answers to your problems or be free from trouble, but you will have a God on your side who remains with you through your trials.

Believe that God is on your side just as he was for Jacob.
Ask God to make himself known to you.
God is never far away from your reach.
*Turn to page 116 to learn more about becoming a Christ-follower.

Day 8: Genesis 33

Jacob wrestled with God and overcame his struggle. Jacob also overcame something else, his fear. Esau was on his way to meet Jacob.

33:1   And Jacob

____
____, Esau was coming, and four hundred men with him.

The female servants Zilpah and Bilhah were placed ahead with their children.

Leah followed with her children. Rachel and her son Joseph came last; likely because Jacob favored Rachel and their son. He wanted to keep them safe in case Esau intended to cause them harm.

33:3   What was Jacob doing as he approached Esau?

33:4-7 How did Esau approach Jacob? What did he want to know?

Likely Esau was riding an animal to meet Jacob. The physical act of dismounting and running to meet someone was not a typical behavior for a man of the culture and region.

Jacob must have been surprised. When he left Esau, twenty years prior, his life had been threatened. Read Esau's emotions and words from Genesis 27:41-45. Write what Esau was feeling when Jacob was home.

33:10   How was Jacob feeling after the initial encounter with Esau?

  For I have ________ _______ ________, which is like seeing
  the ________ ____ _______, and you have accepted me.

33:11   Jacob pleads with Esau to take his gifts and blessings. How did Jacob turn the focus to God? What did Jacob recognize about God?

Twenty years prior, Jacob left his home and livelihood. He spent his life serving his conniving father-in-law for nothing. God blessed Jacob with all he needed to return home, just has God promised in **Genesis 28:15**.

Journal – "God has dealt graciously with me…I have enough." Can you say this about your life? Do you recognize that God has dealt graciously with you? Are you content with God's sufficiency? Think, pray, and write about how God has been gracious and sufficient in your life.

33:12-14 What do the brothers discuss about the journey ahead?

33:15   Esau proves repeatedly that he has forgiven Jacob. What do
        his words in this verse show about Esau's changed
        character?

33:18   Esau returns home to Seir, an area south of the Dead Sea.
        Where did Jacob settle and purchase land?

Read **Genesis 12:6-7.** Who also came to Shechem? What did he do
there?

The Bible does not mention Esau again until Isaac's death. Even
though Jacob and Esau reconciled, their descendants were not at
peace. Esau was also called Edom. His descendants, the Edomites,
were idol worshippers or pagans. The prophets Jeremiah and
Obadiah shared a prophecy from the Lord of Edom's destruction.

PRAY: *Genesis 33:11 – "God has dealt graciously with me...I have
enough." God, thank you for dealing graciously with me. Help me
feel your sufficiency and live in your peace, that I have enough.
AMEN*

Day 9: Genesis 34

✓ Pray ✓ Read ✓ Take Notes

**This is a difficult chapter to read. Feel free to skip this day if you have personal trauma surrounding defilement, human trafficking, or abuse.

This is our first glimpse into the lives and personalities of Jacob's children. Dinah is Leah and Jacob's youngest child. Out of eleven sons, she is Jacob's only daughter.

God had a covenant with Abraham. Isaac was not allowed to marry from the region he lived in with Abraham. A servant was sent to find a wife among his brother's family. Rebekah, Laban's sister left her family to marry Isaac. Esau disobeyed and married from the women of Hittite's, but Jacob was sent to Haran to marry from Rebekah's family. Although marrying family is not a common (or approved) practice today, it was necessary to marry those with the same faith, morals, and belief system. While Dinah's intentions may have been innocent, her family would have impressed on her the importance of marrying within their faith.

34:1-4 Who saw Dinah and what happened?

Dinah's family was camped outside of Shechem (33:18). She was likely a young teenager around age fifteen. Living among so many men, she went out to meet some of the women of the area in Shechem. Some commentaries believe she went to a festival where she would have met the prince. She could have been shopping in the marketplace when the prince spied her.

38

Regardless, this was *no excuse for the defilement. She did not deserve her fate.*

Do not believe the enemy's lies that say
you deserve what happened to you.

34:5-7 Compare Jacob's reaction with his sons':

Daddy's Reaction	Brothers' Reactions

What about their reactions surprise you? What reactions do you feel are justified?

34:8-12 What did Hamor, Shechem's father, offer for Dinah's marriage?

In **Genesis 29:18,** how long did Jacob work and wait for Rachel?

The wedding "night" happened *after* the wedding ceremony, after Rachel's father had agreed to their marriage arrangement.

Shechem had already taken Dinah *physically* as his wife without her consent or the consent of her family. He not only defiled Dinah, but also brought trauma to her family. Therefore, it was so important for those under the covenant of Abraham to remain within their culture for marriage.

34:13-17 Who takes action to avenge Dinah? What is the plan? What is the condition of the marriage?

These sons and grandsons of renowned deceivers (Rebekah, Laban, and Jacob) take control without consulting their father or Leah.

In **Genesis 17:9-14**, God made a covenant with Abraham. A covenant is stronger than a promise. A covenant is made with God and the conditions are enforced by God. A covenant can only be broken by death. God's covenant with Abraham was for Abrahams' descendants to number the stars and receive land for their nations, an everlasting possession. As a symbol of this covenant nation, the men would be circumcised and all baby boys, eight days old. The covenant becomes a part of the body.

The circumcision, part of a sacred covenant, was being used as retribution not as God intended.

34:18-24 Circumcision was a small price to pay for all the men of
          Shechem were promised. What did they assume they would
          have along with women of Jacob's family?

34:25-26 What did Simeon and Levi do while the men of Shechem
          were recovering?

34:27-29 The remaining brothers came and continued their
          revenge. What happened?

34:30   How did Jacob respond to his sons' actions?

34:31   What was their reply?

It is difficult to determine right and wrong in complicated situations.
It seems that fingers could be pointed in every direction. The prince
should not have defiled Dinah. The brothers should not have killed
the men. Jacob should have dealt with the situation so that his sons
did not feel the need to avenge their sister.

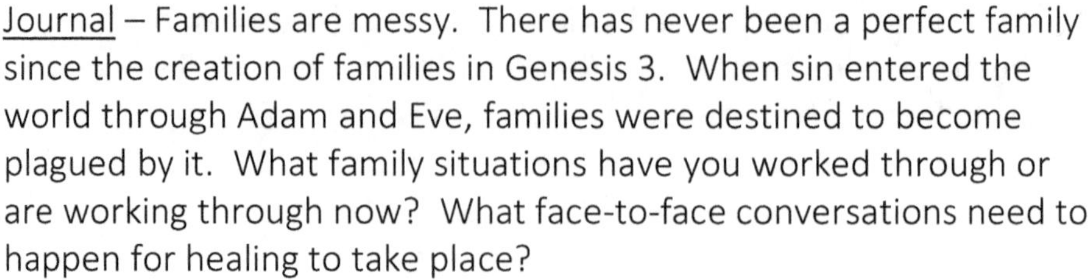

Journal – Families are messy. There has never been a perfect family since the creation of families in Genesis 3. When sin entered the world through Adam and Eve, families were destined to become plagued by it. What family situations have you worked through or are working through now? What face-to-face conversations need to happen for healing to take place?

There may not be a right or wrong answer. Emotional boundaries may be necessary to heal relationships and move forward. Consider seeking counseling to help process family challenges.

PRAY: *Genesis 34:5 – "Now Jacob heard he had defiled his daughter Dinah."* *God, protect our sons and daughters. Protect their minds and bodies from the dangers of sin. Keep them away from ungodly influences and outside predators. Help us teach our sons to care for women with respect and dignity. AMEN*

Day 10: Genesis 35

✓ Pray   ✓ Read   ✓ Take Notes

Jacob's sons caused an uproar in Shechem. Their act of avenging the defilement of their sister, Dinah, by killing, plundering, and capturing the inhabitants, resulted in discord among their tribe and the people of the town.

35:1   What was God's command to Jacob?

The first day of this study we read about Jacob arriving at Bethel. Jacob fled from Esau and found himself alone for the first time. God came to Jacob in a dream, revealing his covenant with him in **Genesis 28:15-22**. What was God's promise? What was Jacob's vow?

After staying on the periphery regarding Dinah's attack, Jacob steps up as father and leader of a nation.

35: 2-3 What does Jacob command his family to do?

Put away _________________ __________ that are among you and _________________ _____________________ and change your garments.

Then, let us arise and go up to _________________, so that I may make there an altar to the God who _____________________________.

The household obeyed and Jacob placed the foreign gods and rings under a tree near Shechem. This was a type of spiritual cleansing for the family before moving on to receive God's blessing in Bethel.

<u>Journal</u> – Leaving their past required putting aside any idols or symbols of idol worship. If we want to walk in maturity in our faith with God, we must leave behind all distractions that hinder growth. Focusing too heavily on work, your busy-ness, and wasting an exorbitant amount of time on television or social media can create idols that keep us from walking closer with the Lord. What idols do you need to lay aside, or have you laid aside, so that you can continue to grow and mature in your faith? Pray and ask God to reveal this to you.

Lay aside your idols and walk in the maturity of your faith.

35:5   How did God protect Jacob and his family on their journey?

35:6-8 What two things occurred when they arrived at Bethel?

Jacob was likely reunited with his father sometime before arriving in Shechem. Rebekah's nurse came with her from Haran when she traveled to marry Isaac. As his mother's favorite, Jacob would have been cared for by Deborah, then came to live with him after his mother's passing.

God reaffirms three things with Jacob:

      35:10 His name:

      35:11 A command with a purpose:

      35:12 A promise:

35:14 What did Jacob do in response?

The drink offering was first used by Jacob in the Old Testament. The pouring out of wine onto an altar represented Jacob's recommitment to God's covenant.

As they journeyed from Bethel, Rachel went into labor with Jacob's twelfth son.

35:18 And as her soul was departing, she called his name
      __________   Meaning (online Bible Dictionary):

      But his father called him ___________________.
      Meaning:

Rachel named him for who he *is*. Jacob named him for who he *will be*.

God does not call you as you are. He calls you for who you will be.

35:19   Where was Rachel buried?

35:22   What happened while Israel (Jacob) lived in Eder?

Reuben's behavior was likely exerting his position as first-born; however, it was sinful and will be used against him later in Genesis.

35:27   Where did Jacob return?

Who buried Isaac?

Rebekah died earlier than Isaac but was not mentioned.

PRAY: *Genesis 35:2 – "Put away the foreign gods that are among you..."* *God, show me my idols that keep me from focusing my life on you. Purify me from distraction and busyness. AMEN*

Day 11: Genesis 36

This chapter records where Esau and his family settled after Jacob arrived and buried their father, Isaac. The chapter also serves to prove that Abraham's descendants would continue to number the stars (Genesis 15:5). God's words to Rebekah in Genesis 25:23 come to reality. Two nations were in her womb.

In Genesis 26:34-35, Esau married two women from the region who were Hittites. The marriages were not acceptable to Isaac and Rebekah because these women had different gods and morals. He sold his birthright, lost his blessing, and made an alliance with the Hittites.

36:7   Why did Esau and Jacob divide their families?

36:8   Where did Esau settle?

Esau's descendants became the Edomites. Esau was also called Edom (Genesis 25:30). It became the great nation that God had promised as kings eventually ruled the land.

In the book of Exodus, the descendants of Israel (Jacob) are enslaved by Egypt. One of their own, a man named Moses (who is also the writer of Genesis) is raised up to be used by God to free them from their enslavement. The Israelites travel to the wilderness of Seir, remaining there forty years. They were instructed to respect the people of Seir and the land. The land belonged to their brother Esau, not Israel. Today this is the upper corner of Saudi Arabia and Jordan.

Deuteronomy 2:4-7 *"You are about to pass through the territory of your brothers, the people of Esau, who live in Seir; and they will be afraid of you. So be very careful. Do not contend with them, for I will not give you any of their land, no, not so much as for the sole of the foot to tread on, because I have given Mount Seir to Esau as a possession. You shall purchase food from them with money, that you may eat, and you shall also buy water from them with money, that you may drink. For the LORD your God has blessed you in all the work of your hands. He knows your going through this great wilderness. These forty years the LORD your God has been with you."*

The chapter lists descendants and leaders within the nation of Edom, documenting the fulfillment of God's covenant with Abraham and Isaac.

Esau, though careless with his birthright, became a man of humility who welcomed his brother home with care and complete forgiveness. He became a powerful and prosperous nation who loved his father and buried him with the honor Isaac deserved.

Journal – We have all had times where we have made foolish mistakes or decisions that lacked wisdom. God still has a plan for you and uses your mistakes for your growth and knowledge of him. On this shorter day of study, take some time to pray and reflect on how God has used your mistakes for good. God redeems when we live our lives seeking him.

PRAY: ***Genesis 36:1 – "These are the generations of Esau."*** *God, thank you, that despite my carelessness and immaturity, you still have a plan for my life. Thank you for teaching me and guiding me in your will. AMEN*

Day 12: Genesis 37:1-11

✓ Pray   ✓ Read   ✓ Take Notes

Sibling rivalry, favoritism, and pride take center stage again as Joseph becomes the next protagonist of Genesis. His father Jacob created the problem rather than helped to diffuse it.

37:2   What do we learn about Joseph?

Genesis 30:5-13 Who were Bilhah and Zilpah's sons?

Joseph, at age seventeen, was the youngest except for one younger brother Benjamin. He had ten older brothers and one older sister.

37:2   What type of relationship does Joseph have with the brothers he is shepherding with?

37:3   Why did Israel love Joseph more than the other children?

Commentaries state that Jacob was ninety-one when Joseph was born. The coat was a long-sleeved tunic made of a rich patchwork of colors. Israel did not hide his favoritism, neither did the brothers hide their feelings.

37:4   How did the brothers feel about Joseph?

Ten older brothers did not hide their feelings toward Joseph. Their demeanor with him left no questions. Joseph did not take this into account but allowed his ego to inflate.

Joseph had a dream and felt the need to relay its details to his brothers, which fed their hatred toward him more.

37:6   Describe the first dream.

The brothers respond with two similar questions but with one different word:

Question 1: Reign   Question 2: Rule

What do you think the difference is between these two words?

The brothers asked if Joseph would become royalty and then have control over them. Their hatred escalated.

37:9   Describe the second dream.

37:10   Joseph shares his second dream with his brothers and who else?

How did his father respond?

Commentaries disagree on whether Rachel had passed at this point as written in 35:16-21. Some believe the birth of Benjamin and death of Rachel occurred after 37 since Joseph was the favorite son at this point. Believing he was the only son of Rachel, commentators think that is why Jacob favored him above the other sons.

37:11 The brothers hatred turned to what?

What did Israel do with the information?

Israel did not disregard Joseph's dream but kept it in mind, thinking about it. Israel had experience with visions from God. Perhaps, in the back of his mind, he wondered if his young son was experiencing the same vision as he.

Journal – Have you ever experienced God showing you something in a dream, scripture, or music? God speaks in different ways. The more time you spend reading his word and praying, He will give you direction. Write about something He has revealed to you. If you have never felt God speaking to you, ask Him to help you "hear" what he is saying.

Sometimes what God reveals to us is for our hearts alone. Not everyone will understand what God has to say. Joseph, though favored, lacked spiritual maturity and humility. Praying before speaking is vital in situations like this.

PRAY: *Genesis 37:11 – "...his father kept the saying in mind." God, help me be aware of when you are speaking to me. Help me understand when to stay quiet and think deeply about your truth. AMEN*

<u>Day 13: Genesis 37:12-36</u>

✓ Pray ✓ Read ✓ Take Notes

The chapter continues with jealous brothers who hated their egotistical younger brother. They had enough of his dreams and self-righteous behavior.

37:12   Where were Joseph's brothers?

In **Genesis 34,** what happened in Shechem?

The brothers plunder of Shechem to avenge their sister, resulted in land for their family. This also shows Israel's prosperity as the flock was so large, the brothers travelled sixty miles from home.

37:14   Israel wanted to send Joseph to his brothers. Why was he going?

In 37:2, what does Joseph do to his brothers when they are pasturing?

Joseph's arrival in Shechem will not be welcome due to his past behavior.

37:17   As he was wandering in search for his brothers, where did he learn they traveled to?

The brothers traveled twelve miles north of Shechem to Dothan as their flock of cattle had exhausted the land there.

37:18-20 What did the brothers conspire to do?

The *pit* was a cistern used to collect rainwater. During summer, the pit was dry. Because of its depth and narrow opening, climbing out would be impossible.

37:21-22 Who "rescues Joseph out of their hands"? What does he decide to do?

Reuben is the oldest brother of the twelve and the first son of Leah and Jacob.

37:23   What was the first thing Joseph's brothers did?

The coat represented their father's favoritism became the first object of their anger.

Joseph was thrown into the empty pit.

Turn to **Genesis 42:21**. The brothers discuss Joseph's anguish in the well. How did they describe Joseph?

Joseph was no match for his older, stronger brothers. They ignored his pleas. The plan was to leave Joseph in the pit, to (secretly) be rescued later by Reuben.

37:25   What arrived and where was it headed?

Dothan was located on a trade route where merchants traveled from the east to Egypt to sell their goods.

37:26-27 Judah offers a different option. What does he suggest?

Apparently selling Joseph would sit better on their conscience than killing him.

37:28   What was Joseph's worth?

Leviticus 27:5 – "If the person is from five years old up to twenty years old, the valuation shall be for a male twenty shekels, and for a female ten shekels."

Joseph was sold for the price of a slave.

Matthew 26:14-15 – "Then one of the twelve, whose name was Judas Iscariot, went to the chief priests and said, "What will you give me if I deliver him over to you?" And they paid him thirty pieces of silver.

Exodus 21:32 – "If the ox gores a slave, male or female, the owner shall give to their master thirty shekels of silver, and the ox be stoned."

Jesus was also sold for the price of a slave.

37:29-30 Reuben was not present when Joseph was sold. What question did he ask?

Reuben was the head of their clan. He was responsible for the lives of his brothers. Reuben began to form a plan to explain Joseph's absence.

The robe was covered in goat's blood and was sent by servant to Jacob to identify. His sons were not present to see their father's reaction.

Hatred and bitterness develop roots of apathy.

37:33-34 What did Jacob assume happened to Joseph? How did Jacob   react?

Shepherds were trained to defend themselves and their flock from wild animals. They had the strength and ability to care for and protect their flock (see Ezekiel 34:12, Amos 4:12). King David was a shepherd and boldly proclaimed of his abilities to strike down lions and bears in defense of his flock (1 Samuel 17:34-37). Joseph likely would have had the ability to defend himself in the chance of attack or his father would not have sent him sixty miles away.

37:35   Jacob refused to be comforted by his family, proclaiming:

____

The Message by Eugene Peterson states, "I'll go to the grave mourning my son."

Journal - Favored or not, the loss of a child stays with a parent for their lifetime. While the pain of loss may lessen, the grief remains. I hope you have never suffered the loss of a child, whether in the womb or otherwise. Take time to grieve and share your grief with others. Just as Jacob wept for Joseph, your heavenly father weeps for you and your child. If you have not experienced loss, reach out to someone you know who has. How can you comfort them? Do you have a memory of their child or loved one to relay? Parents are comforted when others remember the life of their child with them.

37:36 What happened to Joseph?

This moment, though tragic, is part of God's providence for the nation of Israel. Through one man, God will save the descendants of Abraham.

PRAY: **Genesis 37:35 – "Thus his father wept for him."** *God, bring to my mind anyone I know who is grieving a loss. Show me how to comfort them during this time of mourning. AMEN*

Day 14: Rest/Catch-up

Feel free to catch-up on lessons or review to prepare for the upcoming week. You can also take time to record character traits of God on page 6.

Reading through Genesis has brought to light how the presence of sin breeds broken people. From the beginning of God's covenant with Abraham, despite living in the covenant, the presence of sin creates a domino effect throughout the families and generations.

Abraham was known for his faith yet allowed fear to keep him from being truthful with Abimelech and Pharaoh.
Had God not intervened, Abraham would have lost Sarah or faced death.

Isaac was determined to make Esau the son of the covenant. He ignored God's words to Rebekah that Jacob would rule over his brother. His open favoritism of Esau caused family strife and constant competition and deception.

Jacob's deception with his brother led to leaving his family to save his life. Determined to take the blessing he felt he deserved, he lied to his father and took what was planned for him. After marrying his beloved Rachel and Joseph's birth, he carried on the act of favoritism with his son. His deep love for Joseph created pain and divisiveness among his older children.

Joseph and his brothers continued the domino effect of brokenness. Pride, jealousy, and hatred produce roots of bitterness that infiltrate the relationships with them. They would each face the consequences of their sin as God uses the most unlikely circumstances to bring them to their knees through his redemption.

We cannot completely escape the legacy of sin and brokenness, but the death and resurrection of Jesus Christ give us a way to work toward healing and wholeness.

Surrender the broken pieces of your life to God so he can rebuild you to have a positive impact on the relationships around you.

✓ Pray   ✓ Read   ✓ Take Notes

Judah, the fourth son of Leah and Jacob has grown sons. A complicated and tragic family story ends with God's redemption in the lives of Judah and Tamar.

38:1-5 Laying aside a culture where Jacob should have chosen a wife for his son, Judah befriended a Canaanite named Hirah. Then Judah married the daughter of an acquaintance through Hirah named Shua. She bore three sons:

        Son #1:

        Son #2:

        Son #3:

38:6   Who is Tamar?

38:7   What happened to Er?

Culturally, when a son dies without producing a child, the next closest relative must marry the widow to continue the family line for the deceased family member.

38:8-10 Why did Onan refuse to fulfill his obligation? What happened to him as a result?

38:11   What was Judah's plan for Tamar?

Judah's wife died and went to visit his friend Hirah.

38:13-14 What did Tamar do when she was told of Judah's visit?
        Why did she do this?

Prostitutes sat at the city gate, veiled. Tired of living with her father in shame as a widow with no offspring, Tamar, in desperation, decided to take her future into her own hands.

38:17   Judah wanted to take her, not knowing it was Tamar. What did Judah agree to do for the veiled woman?

38:20-23 Judah fulfilled his end of the agreement by sending a goat from his flock. What did his friend discover?

        They kept the goat. What did Tamar keep?

38:24   Three months later, what did Judah find out? How did he react?

38:25   What did Tamar reveal?

38:26   What did Judah admit as he faced his sin?

38:27-30 Twins were born to Tamar. Describe their birth.
        Which was born first? Which had the scarlet thread?

Just as with Esau and Jacob, culturally, the firstborn gains the family birthright. Again, the younger would receive the birthright in the lineage of Christ.

Matthew 1:1-3 "The book of the genealogy of Jesus Christ, the son of David, the son of Abraham. Abraham was the father of Isaac, and Isaac the father of Jacob, and Jacob the father of Judah and his brothers, and Judah the father of Perez and Zerah by *Tamar*, and *Perez* the father of Hezron, and Hezron the father of Ram…"

Tamar, a non-Jew, was the first woman to be named in the lineage of Christ in the book of Matthew. She went from a disgraced, childless widow to a woman God used to create the path for the birth of his own son. Even though Tamar made a choice she didn't want to make, whether to have a hope of bearing children or to have revenge on Judah, God redeemed her sinful choices through her children. She built the house of Judah (Matthew 1:1-3).

Ruth 4:12 "And may your house be like the house of Perez, whom Tamar bore to Judah, because of the offspring that the LORD will give you by this young woman."

Ruth also a non-Jew, a Moabitess, was widowed and childless until her kinsman redeemer came in the form of a man named Boaz. Boaz's mother Rahab was also a non-Jew and a prostitute, redeemed by a great God for her great faith (Joshua 6:17). Boaz is in the lineage of Judah and Jesus Christ (Matthew 1:5).

PRAY: ***Genesis 38:29 – "Therefore his name was called Perez."*** *God, thank you for redeeming me for your purpose. No matter my sin, no matter my shame, you bring me out of the pit and place me on my feet to do your will. AMEN*

Day 16: Genesis 39

Joseph was sold to Potiphar, captain of the guard of Pharoah in Egypt. Purchased slaves worked as servants in the home of the owner. Joseph worked for Potiphar for one year. From a favored son to an Egyptian slave, Joseph must prove himself in a foreign land and an unfamiliar culture.

39:2-6 Joseph was a teenager without his family. Who was with Joseph and how was Joseph blessed because of it?

Joseph's upbringing did little to prepare him for his life as a slave in Potiphar's house. Pampered and favored from birth, Joseph had to fully rely on his relationship with God for this new season of his life. Joseph was stripped of his home and family, but nothing could take Joseph's relationship with God.

Even though God did not rescue Joseph from slavery, he was with Joseph throughout his time in Egypt, giving him success in the middle of the trial.

In **Genesis 15:12-16** in a dream, God told Abram (Joseph's great grandfather) what would happen to his descendants, the nation who would number the stars. What will happen to Abram's descendants and for how long?

Joseph is the descendant who begins the journey to the foreign land of Egypt.

<u>Journal</u> – Have you had a time in your life where God is all you had to rely on? Circumstances may have taken you to a place where you had no family or friends to help you. Write about a time where faith and your relationship with God was all you had to lean on.

In **Genesis 37**, what was Joseph's character like? How did he behave?

God wants to develop our character to be more like him. We were made in the image of God, so we should also walk in the character of God. This comes when we are put in situations to test our character so we can grow and produce Godly fruit.

39:7-10 How did Joseph respond to Potiphar's wife?

Joseph refused to sin against who? (2 answers)

How does this response show a change of character for Joseph? What fruit is Joseph developing?

39:11-18 Potiphar's wife made another attempt for Joseph's attention.

What did Joseph do?

This is the second time Joseph was stripped of his outer garment because of the sins of an attacker. His brothers took his colorful coat and sold him as a slave. His master's wife took his slave garment and charged him with misconduct, resulting in imprisonment. A slave would have likely been killed for making advances toward his master's wife. Joseph was placed in prison, not as a prisoner but put in charge of the prisoners. Potiphar was "keeper of the prison" and likely believed Joseph because he chose not to have him killed. Placing Joseph in prison was an act to appease Potiphar's wife.

Joseph remained faithful to God and his master despite his circumstances.

Write 39:21 below:

____

____

____.

39:22-23 How did God's favor benefit Joseph?

As a parent, Jacob made many mistakes, but he raised a son who knew where to turn when his life was out of his control. Joseph had a relationship with the Lord that his brothers did not have. A relationship that gave him favor as a slave and prisoner.

The greatest gift we can give a child is God himself.

Throughout the trials of this life, it is our responsibility to teach younger generations about God. No matter the challenges a person faces, God's presence will make the biggest impact and help them endure.

PRAY: *Genesis 39:2 – "The Lord was with Joseph…"* *God, thank you being with me even when my circumstances are not what I want, I can rely on you to help me through. AMEN*

<u>Day 17: Genesis 40</u>

✓ Pray   ✓ Read   ✓ Take Notes

God's favor was with Joseph, even in prison. He was given authority over the prisoners while he was there. While this may seem like a worse situation than working for Potiphar, Joseph is being prepared for a greater task.

40:1-3 Who came to be prisoners with Joseph? What did they do?

40:4   What was Joseph's role?

During the night, each of the men had a dream. Because Joseph was given the task of attending to them, he was first to recognize the concern on their faces. Joseph not only cared for the men physically, but also cared for their emotional well-being.

Write Joseph's response in 40:8

____

____.

Joseph had experience with prophetic dreams (Genesis 37:5-11), but he was not in a mature place in his relationship with God for God to reveal the meaning of his dreams in the moment. His relationship had now grown to the point that God would help him understand and interpret dreams.

Fill in the chart below with the dreams and Joseph's interpretations:

	Dream	Interpretation
Cupbearer 40:9-13		
Baker 40:16-19		

40:14-15 Joseph had a request of the cupbearer that he did not have for the baker. What was it and why?

40:20-21 What happened on the third day?

40:22 What did **not** happen?

Journal – Have you ever felt forgotten be a friend, family member, or even God? Are you able to look back and see how God was working, behind the scenes for a greater purpose? Ask God to reveal piece of his plan to you in his time. He sees how the puzzle pieces of your life fit together. Trust him.

You are never forgotten.
You are a part of a greater plan God
has not revealed to you yet.

PRAY: **Genesis 40:23 – "...the chief cupbearer forgot him."** *God, thank you for having a plan for my life. Even when I am forgotten by others, you have not forgotten me. Help me trust you that your plan is greater than what I can see. AMEN*

Day 18: Genesis 41:1-36

✓ Pray ✓ Read ✓ Take Notes

Joseph remained close to God in slavery and in prison. God was with Joseph because of his faithfulness. Joseph is about to see how God orchestrated the smallest details of his life for what is about to come.

41:1 After _________ years, Pharaoh dreamed...

Joseph had to wonder what God was doing as he remained in prison overseeing the prisoners for two years. But now Joseph's dreams as a young man and his ability to interpret the dreams of the prisoners were preparing him for this moment two years later.

Describe Pharoah's two different dreams:

Dream 1 - 41:1-4

Dream 2 – 41:5-7

41:8   What was Pharoah feeling when he awoke? What did he do?

But there was none who could interpret them to Pharoah.

41:9-13 Two years later, the cupbearer remembered Joseph. What
        did he describe to Pharoah?

41:16 Pharoah summoned Joseph from the pit or the dungeon.
      What was Joseph's response to Pharoah about interpreting
      dreams?

Pharoah tells Joseph his dreams. Despite being two different
dreams, Joseph tells him that the dreams are "one" or they have the
same meaning. With God's help Joseph interprets the dreams.

41:26-31 What do the seven good (healthy) cows/ears represent?

        Seven thin, ugly cows/ears?

        How severe will the famine be?

41:32   Why were there two dreams with the same meaning?

41:33-36 What suggestions did Joseph make to Pharoah to prepare
          for the seven years of plenty and famine?

Joseph was invited to come before Pharoah. Clean and shaven, he answered the Pharoah's questions about the dreams. His trust in God gave Joseph the courage and boldness needed to tell the Pharoah how to respond to the dreams, without being asked.

Journal – Has God ever given you boldness and courage when you would typically be afraid? Because of our faith in Christ, we can go before God boldness (Ephesians 3:12). When Peter received the gift of the Holy Spirit on Pentecost, he preached to the people with boldness about the gospel of Christ (Acts 2). What area do you need to be bolder in your faith? Do you willingly talk about your beliefs with your neighbors, coworkers, and friends? Ask God to help you be bolder in your relationship with him and in telling others about him.

PRAY: **Genesis 41:16 – "It is not in me; God will give Pharoah a favorable answer."** *God, thank you for living in me through the Holy Spirit. Thank you for the reassurance that I do not have to go through this life alone. You are with me in every action and reaction. Nothing I do is without your guidance. Help me to rely on you in me. AMEN*

Day 19: Genesis 41:37-57

✓ Pray   ✓ Read   ✓ Take Notes

Through God's wisdom, Joseph was able to interpret the two dreams of Pharoah. Both dreams projected seven years of plenty for the land followed by seven years of devastating famine. Joseph boldly gave the Pharoah direction on how to prepare for the coming fourteen years.

41:37-39 What was Pharoah's reaction to Joseph? What did he say about Joseph?

Pharoah listened to Joseph and could clearly see the Spirit of God in him. Pharoah did more than take Joseph's suggestions into consideration.

Think about where Joseph came from to where God brought him to be in this moment. Add to the chart with the details of Pharoah's promotion of Joseph. 41:40-44

Joseph:
Stripped of his family and status -> Sold to Egypt as a slave ->
Servant to Potiphar -> Charged of a crime with Potiphar's wife ->
Thrown in Prison -> Given authority over prisoners ->

41:45   Joseph was also given:

A New Name:

Meaning: the revealer of secrets

A Wife:

An Egyptian daughter of a priest in the temple of the sun god.

Because Joseph was given the ranking and status, he could not refuse the wife, despite their religious differences. She could marry him because of his new ranking in the land.

The signet ring allowed for Joseph to make laws using the ring to stamp the Pharoah's signature.

41:46   How old is Joseph at this point?

Joseph was around seventeen when he went to Egypt.

After 13 years of being enslaved and imprisoned, he is now the second most powerful man in Egypt.

41:47-49 What did Joseph spend the next seven years of plenty doing?

41:50-52 Prior to the famine, Joseph's wife Aseneth gave birth to their two sons. What are their names and meanings?

Joseph's sons may have helped him temporarily escape the pain of his past, but soon he will come face to face with it. Just as God has been with Joseph during his time in Egypt, he will continue to be with him throughout the next seven years.

41:53-57 In the next seven years what happened? What was Joseph
         able to do in his position in Egypt?

At age thirty-seven, Joseph was positioned by God to feed the people of the land. Through many years of difficulty, he remained close to God, trusting him with his life. Joseph knew he had no control over his circumstances. He knew God was in full control.

Joseph's brothers tried to kill him, but God made a way for him to get to Egypt, to fulfill the prophecy given to Abram. He had a purpose for Joseph even though the road was not easy. Joseph trusted in God's plan.

Potiphar could have killed him, but he did not. God made a way for Joseph to be positioned to eventually gain the ear of the most powerful man in the land.

God has placed you where you are right now. You may not understand, and life feels out of control, but God is working out the details. He is moving other people and circumstances into a position to bring his plan and purpose into your life.

Trust Him.

*When everything seems out of control, God is moving
the pieces of your chaos into order.*

<u>Journal</u> – Reflect back over your life. What parts of your past have prepared you for what you are going through in the present? How have you used past circumstances, lessons learned, fruit growth to help you in your life today?

PRAY: ***Genesis 41:52 – "For God has made me fruitful in the land of my affliction."*** *God, thank you for using my challenging circumstances to help me grow fruit in my character. I may not like the chaos that surrounds me, but you are still teaching and molding me for your purposes. AMEN*

Day 20: Genesis 42

✓ Pray ✓ Read ✓ Take Notes

The famine spread into Canaan. Jacob's sons, married with their own families, were still under their father's leadership.

42:1-2 What question did Jacob ask his sons?

What did he command?

Their hesitation was not serving their families or their father well. Help is in Egypt and they had the means to purchase what was needed for the family to survive.

42:3-5 Who went with the caravan to Egypt? Who remained with Jacob? Why did Jacob keep him behind?

42:6 What was Joseph's role in Egypt?

How did Jacob's son's approach the governor?

42:9 Joseph remembered his dreams. Recall the first dream from Genesis 37:7, what details of the dream are becoming reality?

After twenty years, Joseph's brothers did not recognize him, but out of the thousands coming to Egypt to purchase grain, Joseph knew his brothers without hesitation. When you have a close relationship with God, he helps you see things you would not normally be able to see on our own.

42:7-12 How did Joseph treat his brothers?

42:10-13 How did they respond?

Joseph had twenty years to work through any anger, grief, or bitterness he may have felt toward his family. Their presence must have stirred a mixture of emotions in him. While he came across as harsh, Joseph had a motive.

42:15-17 What did Joseph demand?

Joseph then changed his directions after three days.

42:18-20 What was Joseph requesting now?

We cannot forget the presence of God was with Joseph. His early years of service taught him humility and wise discernment. This is not the brash teenager from Genesis 37. This is a man who sought God's direction in every matter of his life. Joseph coordinated seven years of plenty to provide for seven years of famine for this moment in time. He was not about to abandon God's direction.

<u>Journal</u> – Can you look back over your life and see where you sought God's direction and where you did not? As you have matured in your faith and walked closer with God, how has God shaped your response to challenging situations?

42:21-22 After spending three days in prison, Joseph's brothers admit what?

Joseph learned to speak Egyptian while his brothers only spoke Hebrew. He was able to overhear their admission and conversation of the events twenty years prior. Guilt and shame resurfaced because of unrepentance.

42:24   How did Joseph respond to their conversation?

42:25   How did he show mercy?

42:28   How did the brothers respond when they discovered their money had been returned?

Through Joseph, God made them aware of their sin. They could not receive God's mercy through the darkness of their own sin.

The brothers recounted their story to Jacob and after showing him the money that was returned, they were afraid.

Why do you think they were afraid at this point?

Admitting their sin has caused them to *feel* the weight of their sin.

4:36-38 How did Jacob respond?

Reuben stepped up as Jacob's oldest to rectify the situation. He tried to prevent Joseph from being harmed, but he was taken anyway. Now he was willing to sacrifice his own two sons for the return of his brothers. Jacob would not allow Benjamin to leave for Simeon to be returned to him.

The weight of sin brings years of unresolved bitterness and shame if you do not own your sin. No matter how much time passes, it is important to deal with our sin. Growing closer to God brings transformation. His desire is for your life to be transformed from sin, not remain in the same place, never growing or changing.

As previously mentioned, some commentaries state that Benjamin was likely born after Joseph left for Egypt. Joseph's desire to see Benjamin would be more intense if he had never met his brother and realized that his mother had passed.

Journal – Is there sin in your life you have not addressed? Write about an area of sin where you struggle. Give it over to God. Ask him to open your eyes to instances where this unresolved sin is as play. We are not called to live in fear or shame. He wants us to live changed and free.

PRAY: *Genesis 42:28 – "What is this that God has done to us?"* *God, open my eyes to my sin. I repent of unresolved sin in my life. Show me how it impacts my life and where I need to give It to you. AMEN*

<u>Day 21: Rest/Catch-up</u>

Feel free to catch-up on lessons or review to prepare for the upcoming week. You can also take time to record character traits of God on page 6.

Stripped of his family, possessions, and freedom, Joseph entered Egypt with nothing ... except God. He could have chosen to sit in anger and bitterness, but he chose God. God's way, Gods' wisdom, God's comfort.

I read once that God sometimes allows everything else to fall away until He is all you have left. Even at that point, the choice is still yours to walk the path of bitterness or freedom.

Perhaps Joseph could not mature in his faith under the shelter of a doting father. He could not fully trust God with his life when everything was handed to him at his beck and call. Joseph could not grow into the man who would ultimately save a nation unless he learned how to serve with humility and wisdom.

We have all endured challenging seasons. You may be in a place of struggle now. Do not waste this time, wallowing in anger and bitterness. Choose surrender to God's way, God's wisdom, and God's comfort. Allow Him to prune and shape you to continue to grow in your faith.

God used Joseph to save a nation just as he sent Jesus to save mankind. You do not know how God is using your trials to equip you to save a family, a friend, or a neighbor. He is orchestrating the details of your life to use you for his kingdom.

You do not know what God may be trying to prepare you for, but you will need faith, trust, wisdom, and humility to get there. Ask God what he wants you to learn. He will develop in you an abundance of fruit that will inspire others to walk in surrender to Him.

Maturing in your faith requires surrender to the God who has everything under control.

<u>Day 22: Genesis 43</u>

✓ Pray   ✓ Read   ✓ Take Notes

Nine brothers mercifully received sacks of grain to take back to their families in Canaan. Joseph kept one brother behind, in prison, demanding that they bring Benjamin with the to retrieve Simeon.

Jacob told his sons to return to Egypt to purchase more grain. When they returned the first time, Reuben spoke up to plead to his father about taking Benjamin back to Egypt.

43:3-5 This time, which brother speaks up? What did he tell his father?

Israel scolded them for telling the governor about their youngest brother.

43:7   What did the brothers say was strange about the governor's questioning?

43:8-9 What sacrifice was Judah willing to make?

43:10   How much time has passed?

We do not know how much grain they were given, but Judah said they could have traveled there and back twice in the time it had taken them to use up the grain. Egypt is around two-hundred miles from Canaan, at least 10 days on the back of a donkey, about one month round-trip. It has likely been two months since returning from Egypt.

Joseph gave them enough grain to provide for their needs, but not enough to keep them away longer than two months. They would have to decide about returning to retrieve Simeon.

43:11-13 What were Jacob's instructions to his sons?

43:14   What did he hope all the gifts would do?

The brothers traveled to Egypt. Joseph saw they had returned with Benjamin and had lunch prepared for them at noon.

43:18   Why were the brothers afraid?

43:19-22 What did they explain to the steward?

43:23-25 How did he comfort them in words and action?

The Message by Eugene Peterson reads, "Everything's in order. Don't worry. Your God and the God of your father must have given you a bonus. I was paid in full."

Simeon was returned to them.

I cannot imagine how overwhelmed the brothers must have felt. Did they credit God with his mercy and grace? Mercy is not receiving the punishment you deserve, and grace is receiving a gift with no strings attached. They felt the full guilt of their sin against Joseph years ago and repeatedly blamed the recent events on their past. Did they attribute the blessings to God?

<u>Journal</u> – Have you ever been overwhelmed by God's mercy and grace? How has God shown you mercy and grace? We feel the gravity of sin, but do we feel the gravity of His grace?

43:26-28 Joseph came home to receive his guests. How did his brothers come into his presence? What did he ask his brothers?

Recall the second dream in Genesis 37:9-10. How is the second dream playing out in this scene?

Imagine the emotion in the next few verses. The brother Joseph likely never knew was there. The life and family God allowed to be removed from him will be redeemed.

43:29-30 What was Joseph's reaction when he lifted his eyes and
saw Benjamin?

<u>Journal</u> – Has God ever allowed something to be removed from your life and you did not understand at the time, but he returned it to you later? Are you able to reflect and see why it was removed? Pray for wisdom and understanding if this is an area where you struggle.

43:32-34 When Joseph returned, what was interesting about their
seating arrangements? How did the brothers respond?
What was the overall mood?

Joseph did not reveal his identity yet and did not sit with them. They still thought he was an Egyptian. Non-Egyptians, especially nomads, were seen as filth and never allowed into the home of an Egyptian official. Humble Joseph treated his brothers with mercy, grace, and kindness. He served them with nobility.   His forgiveness was made evident even though his brothers did not know this was the man they had treated so horribly. Possibly for the first time in their lifetime they shared a joyful meal together as brothers.

In **John 13**, Jesus eats with his disciples for the last time. Before the meal, he washes their feet. Jews did not touch one another's feet. The role of the foot washer was given to a non-Jewish servant. In humility, Jesus treats them like royalty even though he knows in a few hours one will turn him over to the Roman soldiers, another will deny any knowledge of their friendship, and still others will run and hide. Through his mercy, Jesus forgives their sin before they realize their need for forgiveness.

What if we acted from a place of forgiveness and mercy because we have already been forgiven and shown mercy?

PRAY: *Genesis 43:23 – "Peace to you do not be afraid your God and the God of your father has put treasure in your sacks for you." God, thank you for your abundance. Thank you for your mercy and grace that we do not deserve. Thank you for overwhelming me with your love. AMEN*

Day 23: Genesis 44

✓ Pray   ✓ Read   ✓ Take Notes

Joseph's brothers received God's blessings, but they had not repented for their treatment of their brother years ago. Joseph had not revealed himself to them. He was the "governor" of Egypt. They have felt like the governor's initial treatment of them was God's punishment, but their hearts were not repentant.

44:1-5 What were Joseph's instructions to his steward?

This silver cup was no ordinary cup. Used in ancient practices for divination or fortune telling, stealing this cup is punishable by death or enslavement. Joseph was testing their allegiance and honor to their family, especially Benjamin.

44:6-13 The steward did as he was told. How did the brothers react to the accusation? What reasons did they give for not stealing the cup? What was their reaction when the cup was found?

44:14-16 How did the brothers react when they went before the governor?

44:17 What would be the punishment?

They had already sold one brother into slavery they would not surrender Benjamin.

In Genesis 42, when Jacob's sons first came before the governor, scripture does not identify any one brother speaking for the family. Using "they" makes it unclear that anyone was taking charge of their venture. As the oldest, Reuben should have spoken on behalf of his family. Jacob and Leah's firstborn had originally told Jacob in Genesis 42:37 "Kill my two sons if I do not bring him back to you. Put him in my hands, and I will bring him back to you."

44:18 Which brother approaches the governor and speaks?

Leah's fourth born. Not Simeon, who had just been released from imprisonment. Not Levi but Judah would go before the governor and intercede for Rachel's youngest son.

Recall in **Genesis 29**, Rachel was Jacob's first love, his favorite wife. She bore him two sons. He lost first-born favorite Joseph and Benjamin had taken Joseph's place. Out of devotion and love to his father, Judah stepped forward to intercede, even though the love had rarely been reciprocated.

In **Matthew 1:2,** Judah is listed in the genealogy of Christ.

Genesis 44:18-23 What did Judah recount to the governor?

In **Genesis 42:13**, the brothers had only told the governor that one brother was "no more".

44:20-28 What details did Judah add about Benjamin and Joseph?
        What details did he leave out?

44:33   What was Judah willing to do for Benjamin?

Although they could not admit what they had done to Joseph, they proved they would show honor to their father and to Benjamin by not leaving without Benjamin.

Jacob's sons honored him and loved him even though it was not reciprocated. They had caused him intense grief because of their treatment of Joseph and loved him enough to make sure Benjamin was treated differently. They laid aside their bitterness and any grudges they held to honor Jacob and Benjamin.

Journal – Have you ever had to lay aside your hurt or bitterness to serve the person who hurt you? Have you chosen honor over your own grief?

Serving others despite your pain shows Jesus' grace to someone who may not otherwise know Him. Always draw and enforce emotional and physical boundaries when necessary.

PRAY: *Genesis 44:34 – "For how can I go back to my father if the boy is not with me?"* *God, help me know when to serve and honor those who have hurt me. Help me keep boundaries when needed, but also discern when I should show your love through me. AMEN*

<u>Day 24: Genesis 45</u>

✓ Pray ✓ Read ✓ Take Notes

Judah interceded for Benjamin, unwilling to return to his father without him. Still not admitting what was done to Joseph, Judah fought to honor his father and brother.

Joseph's emotions are real and intense. Moses (the writer) through the Holy Spirit, shares Joseph's grief and tenderness without holding anything back. Joseph poured grace upon his brothers just as God pours grace out on us.

Do not hesitate to return to these verses and reread them with the intensity Joseph must have been feeling.

45:1-2 After Judah's bold intercession for Benjamin, Joseph cannot hold his emotions at bay any longer. How does Joseph react?

45:3   Write Joseph's words here:

____

____

"But his brothers could not answer him, for they were dismayed at his presence."

Other translations say they were *stunned, terrified, fearful,* or *dumbfounded.*

If they were not already afraid because of the previous accusation, stealing the silver cup, they had even more reason to be afraid now. Their brother, who they sold into slavery, was standing before them as the most powerful man in the land.

45:4   Then Joseph admitted to them what they could not:

I am your _________________, Joseph, whom you

_______________________________________.

The brothers knew they had withheld this detail from anyone except amongst themselves. If this man who claimed to be Joseph also claimed to be the brother they sold, then it must be so.

45:5-8 How did Joseph reassure them? Why did God send him?

<u>Journal</u> – Have you ever looked back over a challenging time and been able to see how God's hand was over the events during that time? Think about how God was working. Have you thanked him for his provision and care during that time? How does this change your perspective during the next difficult season?

45:9-13 What did Joseph tell them to do? What did he promise?
        Where would they live?

Goshen is in the plain of the Nile River delta in upper Egypt. In a famine, it is the perfect place for Jacob's family and their livestock. As the Nile floods every year, there was plenty of irrigation and water for the animals. Also, Egyptians looked down on Hebrews and herdsman. The land of Goshen will be separate from the rest of Egypt, for the nation of Israel to grow and thrive.

Although Goshen is not the promised land, God had a purpose for Jacob's family there. They had outgrown the resources in land of Canaan, especially because of the famine.

45:14-15 All of the emotion of the moment culminates in these verses.
> Make some notes about what all these grown men may have been expressing and feeling.

45:16-20 Pharoah heard about what was going on with Joseph's family. He reiterated what Joseph offered his brothers, but also added more directions for Joseph to share. What did he offer?

45:21-23 What else were they given for their travels?

What was Benjamin given?

45:24 Write what Joseph said to his brothers as they were leaving.
Why do you think he felt the need to say this?

45:25-26 How did Jacob respond to his sons' news?

45:27   What made him believe them?

<u>Journal</u> – Has your heart ever been numb to joy? Has your grief or disappointment caused you to not believe truth set before you? What did it take for your spirit to be revived?

PRAY: ***Genesis 45:5 – "God sent me before you to preserve life."*** *God, thank you for going ahead of me, preparing the path for me to walk. Help me see how you are working especially during the darkest days. AMEN*

Day 25: Genesis 46

✓ Pray   ✓ Read   ✓ Take Notes

Joseph was found and his family saved, Jacob begins the migration to Egypt. With his soul revived, Jacob stops in a familiar place to worship and offer sacrifices.

46:1   Where did Israel (Jacob) stop? What did he do there?

What is significant about this place? Look up the following verses from Genesis and make notes about what happened there.

Genesis	Details about Beer-sheba
21:33	
22:19	
26:23-25	
28:10-15	

Beer-sheba was in the Promised Land, although God had not given the land to them yet. Jacob, his father, and grandfather lived there and worshiped there. They saw visions and God spoke. Isaac, Jacob's father, had been commanded not to leave Canaan, where Beer-sheba was located.

46:2-4 What did God tell Jacob in a vision? What do you think Jacob was feeling and needed reassurance from God?

Jacob did not step outside of Canaan, outside of God's will until he got confirmation that it was God's plan for his family to do so. When God said "go", Jacob did not leave anyone behind, just in case things did not work out in Egypt. Everyone went with Jacob to live in Goshen as God commanded.

Journal – Do you rely on God's assurance and peace in your smaller decisions as well as your lifechanging ones? Is there something you need to take to God to make sure you are going in the right direction?

46:5-7 Who traveled to Egypt with Jacob? What possessions did
they have?

46:28   Who did Jacob send ahead to prepare their place in Goshen?

Jacob sent Judah ahead, not Reuben, Simeon, or Levi, but Judah, the son who stepped up to intercede and care for his family. Judah suggested they sell Joseph to the traders on the way to Egypt (chapter 37). Judah sinned against his daughter-in-law (chapter 38). Despite his past, now Judah prepares the way for his family to come to Egypt.

46:29   Imagine the reuniting of Joseph and Jacob. The lost son was
         found. An old soul was fully revived at the sight of his
         firstborn son of his beloved Rachel.

         What do you think Joseph shared with Jacob? What stories
         did he tell?

46:31-34 What does Joseph explain to his father?

Settling in a new country would have had challenges and unknowns
as they become accustomed to a new land and customs. Joseph
reassured his father of his God's protection and his protection as a
leader in Egypt. Even though they would be ostracized by their
nationality and profession, this would further protect their people,
allowing them to grow and thrive, just as God told Jacob in the
vision.

Journal – Have you ever stepped out in faith and God confirms your
path? Perhaps he does not give you a vision, but he also uses his
scriptures, other people, and circumstances to reassure you. How
have you seen this in your life?

PRAY: *Genesis 46:3 – "I am God, the God of your father. Do not be
afraid..."* *God, thank you for reassuring me that you are God. You
are in control and I have no reason to be afraid of stepping out into
the unknown if that is where your path is taking me. AMEN*

Day 26: Genesis 47

✓ Pray   ✓ Read   ✓ Take Notes

Joseph, reunited with his family, brings them to Egypt because of the severity of the famine in Canaan. Jacob is reassured by God that this is part of God's plan. Egypt is a temporary home for the nation of Israel to grow and thrive.

Reread **Genesis 41:37-44**. Joseph was the governor (like a prime minister) of Egypt under pharaoh. What authority did Joseph have from Pharaoh?

41:44 "I am Pharaoh, and without your consent, no one shall lift up hand or foot in al the land of Egypt."

Eugene Peterson writes in *The Message*, "I am Pharaoh, but no one in Egypt will make a single move without your stamp of approval."

One commentary says, "Joseph's authority was to be absolute and universal."

Recall **Genesis 46:31-34**. Joseph brought his family to Egypt with a plan in mind. What was the plan?

Joseph had absolute authority over every person coming into and out of Egypt. He had absolute say over his family moving to Egypt and living in the land of Goshen. God took Joseph to Egypt to develop his character. The once pious Joseph who strutted around in his colorful coat as the favored son of his father, and the one who shared his dreams with his brothers of their bowing down to him, has been given all authority in Egypt. From God foretelling Joseph's future as a leader to Joseph gaining the mantle of leadership, twenty years passed. God did not give Joseph his authority until he had the humility and character to serve well.

47:1-2 In humility and transparency, what does Joseph do?

47:3   What question does Pharaoh ask?

Joseph was wise and discerning. He served with Pharoah long enough to know the first question he would ask his brothers. Joseph prepared them to answer this in 46:34.

47:3-4 How did Joseph's brother's respond?

Pharoah was cautious of outsiders, non-Egyptians, who came to Egypt. His role was to keep his borders strengthened. Positioning Israelites at the border could cause them to rise and join an enemy of Egypt. Goshen was a safe place, away from foreign territory. Also, he needed to ensure that the family held a profession and would not be idle wanderers, livening off the welfare of the land.

Pharoah fully trusted Joseph. He allowed the family to sojourn in the best of the land. He also asked for any of their herdsman to oversee his livestock as well.

47:7-8 Who else did Joseph bring before Pharaoh? What did
          Pharaoh ask?

Today, it is often seen as rude to ask someone's age. During that
time, it is out of respect and reverence to inquire of their years.

47:9   What does Jacob say about his years on this earth?

Jacob then gave Pharaoh a blessing, praying over him as prophet or
patriarch.

Joseph did what was promised, giving his family the best of the land
in Goshen and food for all.

47:13-19 The severe famine continued. What was given in
          exchange for food?

47:22   Who did Joseph exclude when purchasing the land? Why?

47:24   What was required in payment for seed and land?

47:25   How did the people respond?

The people of Egypt had to indenture themselves to survive.
Twenty percent was not a large payment. This was an unfortunate
consequence of the famine, not something viewed has harsh or
cruel.

47:27   What was life like for Joseph's family in Goshen?

47:28   How long did Jacob live in Goshen?

47:29-31 Near the end of his life, Jacob called Joseph to him and
        asked Joseph to promise to do what?

Jacob desired to be buried in the cave purchased by his grandfather,
Abraham. He was to be buried with Abraham and Sarah, Isaac and
Rebekah, and his first wife Leah (49:31).

Placing a "hand under the thigh" is something Abraham requested
of his servant in Genesis 24:2 before sending him to find a wife for
Isaac. This was a covenant between the men and God as the hand
was placed close to the area of circumcision. This was a sign that it
was urgent for Joseph to solemnly promise he would follow through
with his father's request. Since God was involved, there was a
greater impact.

Peterson paraphrases in *The Message*, "Put your hand under my thigh, a sign that you're loyal and true to me to the end."

After speaking with Joseph, Jacob was emotionally prepared to die.

<u>Journal</u> – After looking at the events of Joseph's life and how he was placed in a position to care for his family, how do you see your position in your life now as a place of God's providence?   Do you believe you are walking in God's will or have you made some decisions that have caused you stray from God's path for your life?

PRAY: ***Genesis 47:12 – "And Joseph provided his father, his brothers, and all his father's household with food..."*** *God, I pray I am in your will, on the path you desire for me. While my circumstances may not be ideal, you still have a plan for my life. Help me to be patient and listen for your leading and guidance. AMEN*

Day 27: Genesis 48

✓ Pray   ✓ Read   ✓ Take Notes

Jacob discussed with Joseph his desires for burial. He wanted to be buried with his forefathers in a cave in the field of Ephron in Machpelah in the land of Canaan.

48:1   Joseph has received word that his father was ill. Who did he bring with him to see Jacob? See also Genesis 41:51-52.

1st born: 2nd born:

Joseph's sons were born during the seven years of plenty in Egypt. They are in their late teens at this point.

48:4   What did Jacob recount to Joseph of God's promise to him?

48:5-6 What did Jacob claim regarding Joseph's sons?

Jacob wanted Manasseh and Ephraim to understand they were part of the inheritance of the promised land. Even though they were born in Egypt, in wealth and power, they would be under the blessing and inheritance of God.

48:9-10 Describe the interaction with Jacob and his grandsons.

48:11-12 Israel was overwhelmed. Why? How did Joseph respond?

Once all hope was lost for Jacob, then it was returned to him double what he lost as he was given Joseph and Joseph's sons.

God is a God of abundance.

Journal – In Ephesians 3:20, Paul writes "Now to him who is able to do far more abundantly than all that we ask or think, according to the power at work within us…" God blessed Jacob abundantly more than he could ask or think. How has this proven true in your life? How have you received God's abundance beyond what you have asked or imagined?

48:13-14 Israel begins to bless his grandsons. Where does he place his hands on the boys?

Israel first blesses Joseph. In the blessing we get a further glimpse of the relationship between God and Israel.

48:15-16 What does he say about God and what God has done for him?

What does Israel ask of God?

48:17-18 What displeased Joseph about his father's hand placement
       on his sons?

48:19-20 How did Jacob respond?

Journal – God always goes against culture. Jesus was crucified for going against cultural norms. Does your lifestyle go against cultural norms? Talk to God about the parts of your life that are more focused on the world than on Him.

48:22   What promises did Jacob give to Joseph?

PRAY: *Genesis 48:15 – "God who has been my shepherd all my life long to this day..."* *God, thank you for being my shepherd throughout my life. You have led me to safety, out of danger, where I can receive your goodness. Help me to look to you as my shepherd and not the world. AMEN*

<u>Day 28: Rest/Catch-up</u>

Feel free to catch-up on lessons or review to prepare for the upcoming week. You can also take time to record character traits of God on page 6.

Jacob knows a bit about the father's blessing falling on the younger son. When his mother was expecting him and his twin brother, God told Rebekah in **Genesis 25:23**, "Two nations are in your womb, and two peoples from within you shall be divided; the one shall be stronger that the other, the older shall serve the younger."

When it was time for Isaac to give the blessing, he intended to give it to his oldest son Esau as was the cultural tradition, but Rebekah remembered what the Lord told her. Through deception, Rebekah ensured that Jacob received the blessing from Isaac (Genesis 27).

God is not concerned with what the world says. He is more concerned with a person's character. Perhaps Jacob favored Joseph because God told him of the character and leadership Joseph would one day exhibit. Jacob also saw in Ephraim the character and leadership he would develop. Jacob goes against culture and trusts God.

We are immersed in a world that does not follow God. Each day, we are targeted to think, act, and believe what the world tells us to. God tells us we are to be in the world but not reflected the world.

1 John 2:15-17, *The Message* paraphrase states, "Don't love the world's ways. Don't love the world's goods. Love of the world squeezes out love for the Father. Practically everything that goes on in the world—wanting your own way, wanting everything for yourself, wanting to appear important—has nothing to do with the Father. It just isolates you from him. The world and all its wanting, wanting, wanting is on the way out—but whoever does what God wants is set for eternity."

Reject the world's way and strive for God's way.

Day 29: Genesis 49

✓ Pray   ✓ Read   ✓ Take Notes

Jacob, on his death bed, has already blessed Joseph's sons. He is now preparing to bless his twelve sons. This is a chapter of prophecy showing what the nation of Israel will become. Each son will be a tribe of Israel, the children of God.

One by one, Jacob blesses each son in their order of birth. Make notes about each blessing beside the son's name.

49:3   <u>Reuben</u>

49:4   Why would firstborn Reuben not be given firstborn privileges? (Genesis 35:22)

What does the Bible translation you are using say about the water in verse 4?

Other translations state: unstable, turbulent, uncontrolled, unruly, reckless, boiling over, wanderer

Reuben lost all honor and integrity as a firstborn son. His character was not fit for that role in the family. His tribe would not receive honor of firstborn within the nation.

49:6   <u>Simeon & Levi</u>

49:6-7 Why will Simeon and Levi be divided and scattered?
        (Genesis 34:30)

Simeonites dwindled in number (Numbers 1:23 and Numbers 26:14) after conquering Canaan. They were so small that the other tribes had to absorb them and did not keep their significance.

Levites were also scattered, but because of their obedience and allegiance to God they were designated as priests and divided between all the tribes. They were not given land as a whole tribe, yet God provided for them through the sacrifices and donations from the other tribes. Moses was a descendant of Levi.

49:8   Judah

Judah, whose name means praise, receives the praise from his father that his older brothers did not. We know Judah did not live a perfect life (Genesis 38), but he ultimately honored his father and brother. The scepter would not leave his tribe. The scepter of a king. King David and King Jesus both descend from the tribe of Judah (Matthew 1).

49:13 <u>Zebulun</u>

Zebulun's tribe in Joshua 19:10-16 settled in Canaan near the sea. They would thrive as a tribe of traders.

49:14-15 <u>Issachar</u>

Issachar is compared to a donkey because while capable of doing great things, Jacob sees he will be content with a life of servitude. He will strive for nothing more.

49:16-18 <u>Dan</u>

Dan's tribe may be smaller in number, but they will be powerful as they seek justice. Dan's tribe will grow to be independent and self-sufficient.

49:19 <u>Gad</u>

Gad is a tribe of warriors. They were warlike and 1 Chronicles 12:8 shows their character as "seasoned and eager fighters".

49:20   Asher

Asher shall produce great products and exports. They will be rich in wealth and production.

49:21   Naphtali

Naphtali is described a beautiful and agile warrior. Each part of the tribes of Israel are blessed uniquely to that tribe. All will contribute to the nation of Israel as a whole.

49:22-26 Joseph

Joseph's blessing was the longest, reflecting of the fruitful bounty in the land of his enslavement. He overcame his enemies (Potiphar's wife, prison, etc.). His faith was strengthened through his trials. He represented Christ and the church (believers) well before their arrival. Joshua, Moses' successor is from the tribe of Ephraim, Joseph's son.

49:27   <u>Benjamin</u>

Benjamin, the youngest son, was prophesied that he would be spirited and warlike. The judge Ehud (Judges 3:15) and King Saul (1 Samuel 9:1-2) would come through the tribe of Benjamin.

49:28   How were the blessings given to the twelve tribes?

… blessing each with the blessing ______________________________.

The twelve brothers have spent their entire lives comparing and arguing with one another. Their father's blessings are suitable and specific to each of them.

God does the same thing for each of us. We tend to compare our blessings, lives, abilities with one another. Social media makes it easy to compare, but our blessings and trials are suitable to each one of us. Your specific trial must be endured in order for you to receive your suitable blessing.

God's blessings and trials are suitable to you.

<u>Journal</u> – Have you struggled with comparison? Do you find yourself looking at social media and wishing you had gifts that others have? What blessings has God given you that are suitable to you?

In chapter 48, Jacob arranged the details of his burial with Joseph. He reiterates his desires with the twelve sons.

49:29-30 What are the specifics of the burial site?

49:31   Who is also buried there?

49:33   "… and he breathed his last and was gathered to his people."

PRAY: *Genesis 49:28 – "…blessing each with the blessing suitable to him." God, thank you for the blessings in my life. Help me stay focused on the blessings you have given me and using them for your kingdom, not comparing my blessings to others.   AMEN*

✓ Pray   ✓ Read   ✓ Take Notes

Jacob blessed his sons according to the blessing suitable to each of them. He reiterated his desires for his burial and left this world.

50:1-3 Describe Joseph's reaction to his father's death. Because of Joseph's position, what was he able to do for his father? What stands out to you?

Jacob was not embalmed in the traditional Egyptian process (removal of organs, mummification, etc.). Jacob was prepared for burial by Joseph's personal physicians so that he could be transported to the burial place in Machpelah. Joseph was so respected that many Egyptians mourned with him for seventy-two days.

Joseph went to speak with Pharaoh's servants because those in mourning could not go before royalty. The mourning process involved not bathing, tearing clothes, and placing dirt or ashes on your head.

50:4-6 What was Joseph's message to Pharaoh? What was Pharaoh's response?

Again, Joseph exhibits humility and integrity in his relationship with Pharoah despite leadership position. He was given full power by Pharaoh, but still chooses to go to him and share what his father asked of him.

50:7-9 Who accompanied Joseph on the journey to Canaan?

Jacob was honored and well respected in the region. Joseph was also highly regarded as evidenced by the Egyptians who attended the procession.

During the journey, the processional stopped at a threshing floor. This was a large area where oxen would stomp on the corn harvested from the crops in the region. It would be a place to accommodate the large group of people moving through the region from Egypt. The Egyptians were very loud and demonstrative while grieving so it did not go unnoticed by the people of Canaan.

50:12 Write the verse here:

Jacob's sons honored him. His deceptive early years turned into showing favoritism in his later years, but he was a man who loved God. Despite their past and challenging relationship, they honored his wishes and place of burial.

50:15   Without the presence of their father, the brothers now have
        some concerns about their relationship with Joseph. What
        were they worried about?

50:16-17 What message did they give to Joseph? How did Joseph
        respond? Why do you think he responded this way?

50:18   His brothers did not keep their distance, they came to him.
        What was their posture and what did they say?

50:19-20 Write Joseph's response here:

50:21   What did he promise his brothers? How did he treat them?

50:22-23 What did the end of Joseph's life look like?

50:24-25 What did Joseph tell his brothers? What did he ask of
        them?

50:26   How old was Joseph when he died? Where was he buried?

When the people of Israel leave Egypt after 430 years, led by Moses
and commanded by God to take over Canaan, Joseph's bones are
taken with them into the promised land. **See Joshua 24:32.**

Joseph lived in Egypt for 93 years, serving God, his people, and the
people of Egypt. Because he lived in Egypt, they would not have
allowed him to be buried outside of the country. Each of the
patriarchs of faith (Abraham, Isaac, Jacob, and Joseph) died in faith
that God would fulfill the covenant for the nation of Israel to live in
the promise land. Joseph's coffin remained in view for three
hundred years so he would not be forgotten and would be carried
to the promised land.

Journal – Look at Joseph's life. Think about the negative aspects, his
early behaviors, events that were painful. Think about the end of his
life and how he grew his character. What did he attribute the way
his life turned out? Look at your life. How have you grown despite
trials and challenges? What do you attribute to your growth?

PRAY: ***Genesis 50:20 – "...but God meant it for good."*** *God, help me
trust you that the challenges I face will be ultimately meant for my
good. It may not feel good at the time, but you will use it for my
good. AMEN*

Conclusion

Congratulations on completing part two of Genesis. If you chose to complete part two before part one, I hope you are so intrigued by the story of Jacob and Joseph that you will go back to the beginning to study God's creation, Noah, Abraham, and Isaac.

The patriarchs and matriarchs of the Christian faith are inspiring, frustrating, courageous, and imperfect. Their similarities are as varied as their differences, yet God still chose them. Their imperfections and dysfunctional families give hope to those who are struggling to live and raise families in a crazy world.

It is my hope that you have been able to spend some time reflecting on their stories and how your own story is just as important. We each have significant role in carrying out our faith to a hurting world. While our words are important, our actions shine brighter in the darkness that surrounds us. God has placed you within your story at this time for a purpose. While I am sure there are aspects of your story you wish you could change, God would not change any detail. The events of your life form who you are and impact your faith in ways you may not be able to see in this moment. Keep walking in faith. God sees your struggles but has given you blessings based on your unique character.

At the end of this thirty days of study, look back over your notes and revelations of the character of God. Is God different than you realized? Did you learn more about him than you first thought?

Ideas for Study

church small groups	family study	neighborhood study
women's group	summer study	men's group study
teen or youth study	couples	individuals

Steps for Salvation

If you have never made a decision to follow Jesus or need to refresh your commitment, below are some scriptures and a prayer to guide you into a relationship with Jesus Christ.

Romans 3:23 – "For all have sinned and fall short of the glory of God."

Romans 6:23 – "For the wages of sin is death, but the gift of God is eternal life in Christ Jesus our Lord."

Romans 5:8 – "But God proves his own love for us in that while we were still sinners, Christ died for us."

Romans 10:9 – "If you confess with your mouth, "Jesus is Lord," and believe with your heart that God raised him from the dead, you will be saved."

Romans 5:1 – "Therefore, since we have been declared righteous by faith, we have peace with God through our Lord Jesus Christ."

Romans 8:1 – "Therefore, there is now no condemnation for those in Christ Jesus."

Romans 8:38-39 – "For I am persuaded that neither death nor life, nor angels nor rulers, nor things present nor things to come, nor powers, nor heights nor depth, nor any other created thing will be able to separate us from the love of God that is in Christ Jesus our Lord."

If you believe that these words from the Bible are true, and would like to begin a relationship with Jesus Christ, pray and talk to God. You can use these words to help you:

Dear God,

I know that I am a sinner and nothing I can do will earn my salvation. I deserve death for my sins. Thank you for sending your Son to die as the ultimate sacrifice as payment for my sin. Come in and be Lord over my life. I place my faith and trust in You. Thank you for your grace and forgiveness. Thank you for the reassurance that nothing I can do can ever separate me from your love.   Amen.

If you prayed this prayer, tell a friend or family member who is also a believer. Find a church that can help you grow in your faith. I am praying for you, friend!

To schedule *Leah Lively* for an event, contact:

Leah: leahlivelyblog@gmail.com
Subject: Speaking Inquiry

Possible topics include:
Spiritual Growth
Scripture/Bible focus studies
Integrating God's word into everyday life
Motherhood

Resources and Helpful Links

1 – *The Holy Bible*, English Standard Version, 2001 by Crossway

2 – *The Historical Atlas of the Bible,* Dr. Ian Barnes, 2006 by Chartwell Books

3 – *Rose Book of Bible Charts, Maps, & Time Lines*, 2015 by Rose Publishing

4 – *Layman's Bible Book Commentary*, 1978 by Broadman Press

5 – *Mathew Henry's Commentary*, 1961 by Zondervan

6 – *The Expositor's Bible Commentary Vol. 2*, 1990 by Zondervan

7 – Online Bible & Study tools: https://www.biblehub.com

8 – Bible App: *She Reads Truth*

9 – Online Bible tools: https://www.biblestudytools.com

10 – *The Basic Bible Atlas: A Fascinating Guide to the Land of the Bible*, 2020 by John A. Beck

Meet Leah Lively

Born and raised in Virginia, Leah's faith journey began in a small loving church in a small town. Through multiple moves and life-altering events, Leah has clung to the Word of God as her lifeline when everything else seemed to be disappearing. Her passion is Second Corinthians 13:11 where Paul encourages the church in Corinth to "become mature and be encouraged, be of the same mind, be at peace, and the God of love and peace will be with you." She wants believers to grow in their faith and discover a hunger for God's word.

Married with four kiddos and a menagerie of pets, Leah finds time to write on her self-titled blog, speak, and publish articles online. Leah's genuine and authentic style of presenting the gospel lays a foundation for readers to learn more of God's truths.

All of Leah's studies are available on Amazon and her website.

Connect with Leah online:

Website: https://leahlivelyblog.com
Facebook: Leah Lively Blog
Instagram: @leahlivelyblog

Praise for "30 Days with John: A Journey with Jesus' Most Beloved Disciple"

"Has reading the Bible ever seemed a daunting task? Do you have trouble remembering dates and historical facts? Do you long for a better understanding of God's Word? Sometimes even my best attempts to study and retain information leave me grasping to remember details.

In Leah Lively's book, "30 days with John, A Journey with Jesus' most Beloved Disciple", you are invited to focus on one book of the Bible. This approach helped me to retain information vital to my faith. It offers such a warm approach to truly learning about a man, John, who walked and talked with Jesus. The summaries at the front of the book help give a visual image of how life was for them during this time.

Daily devotions help the reader to get to know John, Jesus, and begin to internalize this amazing book of the Bible. What a great way to learn about our Lord and Savior!"

Beth Townsend, *Life on Purpose TV*

Amazon comments:

"I like how Leah helps us to study and examine what John had to say with wisdom, grace, and a laser focus!"

"There are thought provoking questions that carry you through each chapter of the book of John."

"Each day can easily be completed in 20-30 minutes. There are great reflection questions, totally focused on the Bible and not fluff."

"It is written so that if you are a new Christian, or a 'seasoned' Christian, you can understand and get to know John's biblical journey in just 30 days."